The item should be returned or renewed by the last date stamped below.

Dylid dychwelyd neu adnewyddu'r eitem erbyn y dyddiad olaf sydd wedi'i stampio isod.

Newport
CITY COUNCIL
CYNGOR DINAS
Casnewydd

To renew visit / Adnewyddwch ar
www.newport.gov.uk/libraries

THE UNION OF SYNCHRONISED

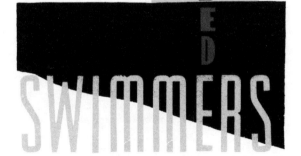

SWIMMERS

cristina sandu

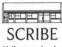

SCRIBE

Melbourne • London

Scribe Publications
2 John St, Clerkenwell, London, WC1N 2ES, United Kingdom
18–20 Edward St, Brunswick, Victoria 3056, Australia
3754 Pleasant Ave, Suite 100, Minneapolis, Minnesota 55409, USA

Originally published in Finnish as *Vesileikit* by Otava in 2019

First published in English by Scribe in 2021 by arrangement with
Rights & Brands

Text copyright © Cristina Sandu 2019

Translation copyright © Cristina Sandu 2020

Typeset in Adobe Caslon Pro by the publishers

Printed and bound in the UK by
CPI Group (UK) Ltd, Croydon CR0 4YY

Scribe Publications is committed to the sustainable use of natural
resources and the use of paper products made responsibly from those
resources.

9781913348236 (UK edition)
9781922310163 (Australian edition)
9781950354399 (US edition)
9781925938333 (ebook)

Catalogue records for this book are available from the National Library
of Australia and the British Library.

scribepublications.co.uk
scribepublications.com.au
scribepublications.com

Crane, porpoise, flamingo, dolphin —
beings that live in or by water. These
are also the names for positions in
synchronised swimming, performed
seemingly effortlessly, on the threshold
between floating and sinking.

When spring came, the girls were the first at the river. They left their clothes in bundles on the bank, stretched their bodies in the sand, and ran into the water. The coldness was sharp. They smoked with just their heads above the surface, blew smoke into the sky, and laughed with their necks bent back. Ash scattered on the water, which held their white breasts like doves.

There were empty soda bottles, egg shells, chicken bones gnawed bare, bread crusts, and cheese that had melted, cooled, and then congealed, all scattered across the picnic blanket. A yellow tractor stood in the mud close to the bank. A hen was laying eggs behind the wheel. A pig was bathing in the river. Farther out were six other swimmers.

The girls started to play, though they were too old; their movements aimless at first, like they could've been doing anything else. They plunged into the water and sprang up, parting the surface with their hands. They crept among the reeds and made birds scatter from their nests. They tore flowers growing by the river and drew shapes in the air.

They pushed each other's heads under the surface and kept them there, as if performing a baptism. They stood on their hands in the water, their feet swinging madly against the branches of the trees.

Now, there are places that are on the wrong side of the river and places that are on the right side. When the girls sat on the shore, they looked from the wrong side across to the right side, on the bank of which a wharf reached forward.

The land where the girls lived didn't belong to any country. Its name meant The Near Side of the River. Its beauty was the only kind they knew. The cement buildings of the city, the blue-roofed monastery at the top of the only hill, the war memorials and the stony Lenins that had escaped demolition after the fall of the Republic. The profiles of the metal and cigarette factories which would grow huge at night and loom over the houses. The pigeons and dogs that ambled through the streets. The town belonged to them, too. It was surrounded by green and yellow fields, other towns with little cottages, forests, meadows, and the river.

But a silence pervaded the land: for most of the year, the men were gone. They grabbed any kind of work they managed to get in a neighbouring country. They sent letters and packages home, and came to visit

when they had enough money or their homesickness had become too great.

Only the women stayed. They kept life going. They worked the land, fed and slaughtered the animals, raised the children. They ensured that the metal factory filled the sky with red smoke. They prepared the cigarettes, crammed neatly into elegant white packs, which then went on to fill glistening cartons to be shipped far away, by land or by sea.

ANITA, HELSINKI

ANITA, HELSINKI

I meet Blue Flame a bit before the summer solstice. I'm sitting on the steps of the cathedral, leafing through a book of Finnish grammar, when I feel a presence near me. He sits down casually, his dark blue wings settling calmly around him. He looks at me every now and then, not intrusively but tentatively.

Hello, he says. Because of the mask, his voice comes both from nearby and far away. He leans his golden upper body forward and presses his palms against the edge of the step.

What's up?

I close the book. My fingers are shaky. I'm sure I recognise his accent. I stick to English, the shared foreign language a bulwark between us.

I'm good, thank you.

What's your name?

Anita, I say, pulling the hem of the dress over my white knees.

Tell me, Anita, are you from here?

He clearly hasn't seen the book I'm reading, but what matters is that his question proves I look like someone who could belong here. The truth is, I've lived in Helsinki for almost a year, but the city feels as strange as it did when I arrived.

I've moved around my whole life. I don't really feel like I have a home anymore, I answer cryptically. But I'm trying to find it, I add.

He has a pensive look. People need stability, he says, as he lights a cigarette. He offers me one, but I refuse with a nervous hand gesture.

This year I have been to six countries and eighteen cities, he says, laughing.

Blue Flame, the Hunter of the Skies, Gold as the Sun and Blue as the Day, has hung from the Eiffel Tower and done cartwheels at the Piazza del Popolo in Rome. He was swinging from the trees along the Thames in London when an agent asked him to star in a television ad. He ended up dancing in the middle of a crowd while chocolate bars fell from the sky.

I look at him, the hero of my childhood cartoons;

the thin, glossy fabric stretches over his body, golden except for the beak and forehead, which are the same blue as the wings. His eyes are two narrow, dark holes. He has rolled up the mask above his thin lips.

When Blue Flame suggests we go for a drink, I have a chance to refuse and get rid of him. I don't need any reminders of what I've left behind. I have a lot to read. I bite my lips. Then I say: Yes. Why not.

As we walk across the square, I feel self-conscious of the fact that I'm walking next to a superhero and people are staring.

How does it feel when people stare? I ask.

Of course they stare! Blue Flame says. He has taken his mask off and now his voice sounds ordinary. The mask has left red marks on his forehead and cheeks, and his short hair is standing up. His face is long and covered with acne scars.

It's part of the job.

We find a bar in a quiet alley, at the end of which a slice of the sea glares at us. We choose a table by the window.

The long, pointy wings hang elegantly on the back of the chair. The golden gloves lie on the table. Blue Flame is excessively cheerful when talking to the waitress: Some chicken wings, please?

I pass on the chicken wings but order a beer. Blue Flame slowly pronounces the name of our home country and nods. A tiny piece of land by the river. A country that isn't even a country. My palms begin to sweat, and I rub them against the hem of my dress.

People end up there by accident or because they have no choice, he explains. Most want to leave but cannot. My family is stuck there, you see, like a broken train.

But you aren't, I say, trying to shake the tension out of my voice.

No. I thought: why not leave, I am ready to do anything to get away. And whenever I feel like it, I will go back, he says.

If I blush, he doesn't seem to notice. I drink several glasses of water and chew on the ice cubes. I blink my eyes furiously to moisten my contacts.

So you were born here? he asks.

I could still say: No. I too left the place that everybody wants to leave. Instead, I hesitantly shake my head and lie about my parents. Artists, both of them, always on the move, I say, and wave my hand to wipe away distant memories.

As soon as the waiter places the beer on the table, I take a big gulp.

Where I'm from, everything is small and limited, Blue Flame says after a while, and dips a chicken wing carefully into the barbecue sauce. It's a place not good to people, he continues, and laughs dully, only to dogs.

I stretch my hands on the table, my nails like pink almonds, clean and symmetrical. His tanned fingers are fiddling with a small cross hanging from his neck.

I drink some more and feel relaxed. What brought you to Helsinki, I ask, of all the northern cities?

He sighs, taps his plate with the fork, and dramatically says: Longing.

I look at him. He shrugs, suddenly exhausted. He opens his mouth, then changes his mind and stays quiet. I wonder whether I dare order a second pint. Back home, women drink moderately, and mostly fruit wine.

He says in a half-whisper: I started to feel I was choking. Like I was living inside a box.

Something stirs in me, a form of compassion or recognition. Then I hasten to nod. I order a second pint, like women here do all the time.

Even though it's been a while now since I left, hearing my mother tongue always puts me on edge. Instead of warmth I feel annoyance, as if the language is mocking me. And so we go on talking

in English. The moment I could naturally tell him I speak the same language — his, our language — slides past.

The next day, I go for a long walk by the sea. The city seems kinder. At the marketplace I buy tiny fish wrapped in newspaper and eat them as I stroll by the cold green water.

On my way back to the city centre, I notice the gold and blue at the Senate Square. A few children have stopped to stare, and their parents awkwardly try to hurry them. Blue Flame is focused on his movements. He stands on his hands for a long time, then on one hand, spreading his legs slowly into an L-shape, one ankle skyward. The crane. Then he comes down to stand on his head and raises his arms in the air. He seems utterly separate from the landscape, as if glued onto it, and yet everything adheres to him: pavement, ice-cream truck, passers-by. I keep walking.

Last night, after many beers, we took this same street to the tram stop, where our paths forked. Blue Flame had lifted the mask onto his forehead like a headband, so four eyes were watching me. He ran his fingers gently along my waist — but then the tram

arrived, and when I stepped inside, he pushed me gently with his fingertips, sending me off. As the tram moved away, I still felt watched, by his own eyes and the eyes on the mask.

It's late at night and Blue Flame is leaning against the window sill. He looks around and takes a drag from a cigarette.

So, this is what the home of a Finnish intellectual looks like, he says in an ironic tone.

He has taken the mask off completely but is still wearing the costume. There's nothing Finnish in my flat, nor anything from my own country. Ten months haven't given it the slightest personal touch. There isn't even a bookshelf — only heaps of papers and books piled up.

I pace nervously in the space between the fridge and the table. I arrange olives and pickles into small bowls. I glance at the mirror and straighten an eyebrow with my little finger. Nobody has been here before.

Relax, Blue Flame says.

He dumps his cigarette in the one flower pot I own — filled, but only with soil — and lays his fingers

on my arm. I take my face away from the mirror and turn to him, careful not to move my hand.

The fingers close around my wrist like tentacles. Blue Flame's kiss is long, strong, and tastes of nicotine. He takes off his costume and places it carefully on a hanger, like he lives here. Then he puts his hand under my skirt. Suddenly two fingers are inside. Clothes drop on the floor like uncertainties. I bite my lip so that words in the wrong language don't spill out. We are about to fall on the bed when I command him, surprised by my own voice: Put the mask on. He gives me an annoyed glance. I avoid looking into his sweaty, dark face. He fetches the mask from the window sill.

First his fingers lay on my neck, then curl around it, simply holding it. Then they squeeze. I wriggle to break free. Meanwhile he's moving inside me, like he's trying to get somewhere. His short beak pecks rhythmically at the air. My body, exhausted, becomes still. I look into his deep, unblinking eyes. I start to think about the dim lamp of my childhood bedroom, spotted by disgusting flies. I try to speak but there's no air in my throat. Anyway, I wouldn't beg him to stop. I would urge him to go on. Продолжай, I'd say, as gently as I could.

The next evening, I only notice Blue Flame after I have arrived home, walked into the kitchen, and opened the fridge. I'm just about to grab a yoghurt, my eyes worn down by vocab lists, when I see him there, standing nonchalantly by the window. Did he climb through the window, up the branches of the pine tree?

He's smoking. The tiny butts building up in the flower pot look like abnormal carrot sprouts. I open the window wide and let the white-summer night sky enter. He gives me a bouquet of sunflowers that I place in water glasses around the flat. He has also brought French fries, which we eat sitting on the window sill. Afterwards, he puts on familiar songs, like 'On the Hills of Manchuria', and I tell him how lovely they are and turn the volume up. We dance a bit. The summer night goes on like a waltz. He checks out of his hostel the next morning and brings his suitcase to my flat.

I lie on a picnic blanket surrounded by birches. Blue Flame talks about our home country with a mixture of anger and tenderness. Maybe distance has made the latter grow. He does not hide or decorate. His words make me want to talk about it too: the smell of boiled apples, the horses, the bends in the river. The need to

speak grows inside me, but I stay quiet and gaze at the bright green leaves against the sky.

I'm about to fall asleep when he begins to tell me about migrating olive trees: Like people, trees migrate, from one country, one continent to the other! This particular species of silvery olive trees, he explains, has spread across the Americas, but the first sprouts were brought by some homesick Eastern European settlers.

When I pronounce his name, I do it slowly and clumsily, like I am declining a Finnish verb.

Anita, now it is your turn to tell me something, Blue Flame says.

He's obviously right. He has spoken so much his voice is hoarse. He sits with his legs crossed, playing with a lighter. I sit up and anxiously brush my new blonde hair. I don't know what to say, so I recite a poem: the one about the science of departures. Blue Flame's eyes are glowing when I say the last line. He wipes his nose with his hand.

How do you know that poem? he asks.

I love Osip Mandelstam, I tell him. I've read everything. In English, of course, but the translations seemed excellent.

The intensive language course I enrolled in turned out to be a great idea. Not only am I starting to grasp little details about the language, but it's comforting, too: my feelings of loneliness are normal. To actually find a place inside this culture is hard, but possible. People have done it before.

In the meantime, Blue Flame is becoming increasingly nervous and disappointed. His mood changes abruptly, depending on tiny details, like a misplaced word or accidental laughter. If I forget to buy something he specifically asks for — vinegar, apple juice, mint tea — he calls me names I'd forgotten and which fill me with shame. He's counting his money now and staring gloomily into the distance.

Summers are the best working time for a superhero, Anita. I can't waste my days like this.

He's been squatting in my place for a month.

His voice breaks as he pulls at his hair restlessly. He jumps into the gold-and-blue costume and storms out of the room. I stay lying on the bed with just the sheets around my body.

One afternoon a few days later, he comes back cheerful and smelling of cologne. I'm too busy practising Finnish cases, so I ignore him. He puts music on. The horses of a war battalion gallop through

the room and cut across my thoughts again and again, until I realise I can't read anymore.

I can't read! I shout. Then I repeat it deliberately, looking into his small eyes.

He's frozen in the middle of the flat. I say his name, but this time as if it were a nuisance. He takes a step towards me. I curl up even more on the sofa and bring the book close to my face.

But my little flower … Blue Flame blabbers awkwardly. His wings drag miserably on the floor.

I don't put the book down. He paces indignantly around the flat. He stops in front of the open window, stretches, and climbs onto the window sill. Slowly, he starts to bend himself into the position I've seen him do at the Senate Square. Soon half of his body is outside the window. I scream, rush to him, and force him back in. We stand opposite each other: he hugs me, I slouch.

You've become very cold, he says, in a deeply wounded voice.

I lean my head against his shoulder and whisper how sorry I am. I breathe in, trying to fill my lungs with the sweet smell of apples before it disappears.

Little flower, Blue Flame says again, cringing.

He puts the mask on and we fuck on the floor, like

stray dogs do back home, on the edge of the field. I hear my voice from far away when I suggest that we change positions. I'm too old for this, I laugh. That's when he clutches my hair and bends my head back. He seizes me from the hip. My knees scratch against the floor and his fingers dig into my skin. I stay still like furniture, so it hurts less.

I've decided to leave, Blue Flame mumbles.

I'm chopping chanterelles I picked from the island during the solstice. The movement of the knife slows down but doesn't stop.

Oh, really?

He clears his throat. First to Denmark, then Norway, he says. And then home. My visa expires soon. I will probably never be back.

Chop, chop, says the knife, and stops. A clod of butter sizzles in the pan.

Blue Flame takes his costume from the hanger and begins to fold it with exceedingly slow movements. Something twists inside me. I throw the chunks of mushroom into the pan. Before you leave, do tell, has the city grown, the river shrunk?

But I don't say that. Even if something inside me

is seething, I calmly shake the pan. My voice doesn't even tremble when I say: Иди нахуй.

What? he asks.

He takes a few steps towards me. His whole demeanour is alert. Then something painful spreads across his face. His eyes narrow, lips squeeze together, and he raises his fist.

I'm ready to take whatever is coming, but something pierces Blue Flame's anger and makes his hand fall.

Bitch, he says, closes his bag, and leaves.

I can see him walking down the street, smaller and smaller. I put the knife down. I'm about to open the window to call him. Then I notice a sprout in the pot among the cigarette buds: tiny, pale green, and askew.

The girls' bodies mingled in the water. Hand touched hand, foot grazed foot, fingers entwined. A pair of glasses lay in the grass, purposeless. The sun bounced off their metal rims and off the haughty earrings the bathers hadn't removed. One of the girls had extremely long, thick black hair that wrapped around her neck and arms like a net. Another had a ring on her ring finger: a silver-red circle that sank into her plump flesh. She was called Adidas because she had a pair of red trainers from across the border.

They were not yet in possession of their movements. The river did what it wanted with them. Algae reached for their legs from the bottom. They swallowed a lot of water which tasted like mud and fish.

The land across the river was known as The Far Side of the River. For a while, The Far Side had tried to hold on to The Near Side, but it refuses to belong to anyone to this day, and hence does not really exist.

The Near Side of the River is governed by the Captain, who ensures that the shops have food and clothes, and the cars have petrol. That the metal factory keeps running.

That there's news on the TV and light in the lamps. The Captain owns the prolific tobacco factories. These produce an incredible amount of quality cigarettes, which in the neighbouring countries are as popular as fish eggs and brandy. They are called Cheap Whites.

The girls worked in the factory where the tobacco leaves were crushed, condensed, and swirled into excellent cigarettes. In the evenings, their weary eyes fixed on the TV: melodramas the whole town followed. Sex, tears, murder. Then, one day, when it was still winter and everything smelled of burnt wood and the girls were nibbling at salami and drinking spritz, a swimming pool appeared on the screen. The girls poured more spritz and turned the volume up. On the TV played a documentary about a new sport involving women who were no ordinary swimmers. First, they floated separately, looking at each other from different sides of the vast pool, and seemed to mimic each other's movements: arms lifted, crooked, opened. Their legs pedalled the water, keeping the rest of their bodies afloat. Then, calculated gestures began to cut through the water and the blue between them shrank until they formed one body: it plunged deep and started to rotate, slowly, with no need of air.

The day The Near Side of the River celebrated its anniversary, the girls weren't singing the national anthem in flowery dresses, nor were they doing cartwheels in front of tanks decorated with flags. They were performing in another kind of show: they skipped rope by the river, touched their toes with their fingers, and leaped into the water, splashing furiously. Every once in a while, they turned on their backs and floated. They were as inseparable from the river as the reeds and the stones.

As summer advanced, there began to be something determined and aggressive about their movements, no longer mere play. The girls honed their bodies relentlessly. Their skin shaded into bruises. They ran along the riverbank, bend after bend. They stretched into new positions in the water; sometimes hands, sometimes feet above the surface.

Maybe they imagined they were stars, or angels, or insane birds. Sometimes they grabbed each other's hands and legs and twisted them so harshly that it was a miracle nothing broke. They tried to straighten their ankles, which curled instead. The bodies, striving to float, sank helplessly. They cursed their breasts, heavy in water.

The girls spent more and more time underwater. The pressure in their ears started to disappear. To the uninitiated, it seemed they were trying to drown

themselves. When they all squatted in the water with just their hands above the surface, it looked like they were praying.

Then the black swimming suits appeared. Goggles and bathing caps. Waterproof lipstick. In a non-country, there's nothing one can't buy or sell. Goods come and go; hidden at the bottom of cars, inside the wheels, and between the doors. The only limit is one's imagination, especially with Cheap Whites as currency. Would you like red or blue tennis shoes? A Winchester rifle? A Glock? A censored novel? Weight-loss infusion? Morning-after pills, a puppy of a noble breed, a peacock, the seed of a rare orchid? The most flexible bathing caps and compact goggles?

The swimming suits fit perfectly. When their thin fabric settled on the girls' sunburnt skin, something clicked.

They were sitting by the river, swinging their legs in the water and sucking on the tips of their hair. They knew how to do this — they had seen it on TV. They took a deep breath, tensed their bodies, and dived. Like fish, they vanished under the water. Then, six pairs of feet appeared above the surface, but this time with nicely stretched ankles. Their legs bent, back and forth, like herons.

They gasped.

The air was heavy. The voice of a rooster broke the

silence, then quickly grew quiet. The smell of mud, water lilies, and dung condensed. Around the river, the parched land radiated thirst. Something dark and heavy was looming in the sky. The girls pulled up onto the bank, dried themselves, and dressed. The glasses returned to the freckled nose and details became clear again. Before leaving, they gathered behind a tree and whispered cheerfully, glancing around. The swimming suits hung from the branches like crows — like fateful omens, people would say, but only afterwards.

PAULINA,
SAN LUIS OBISPO

Paulina stands on the deck of the boat. She watches the diminishing port of San Luis Obispo: her almost-home looks strange from this perspective, tiny houses squeezed between the sky and the sea. The wind is pulling at her black, high ponytail, entwining it around her neck. She thinks she must look like a plump raspberry in her pink raincoat — one that is about to roll into the sea.

This morning she stormed out of her house just to be anywhere else for a day, but now she realises that she's enjoying it. The sea gives her a thrilling feeling that has something to do with escape. For a few hours, she has nothing to care about. She imagines the boat

leaving behind not only the port but also the small rooms of her house, the wrinkled sheets still damp with the sweat of bodies.

The port is eventually swallowed up by the horizon. Spume shoots up from under the boat towards the sky. A sailor walks along the deck collecting money in a can. At the end of the day, the one who has caught the biggest fish will win the whole pot. They call it the lottery.

Paulina peels the rod out of the bag and weighs it in her hands. Her fingers close around it. The gesture feels familiar, even if she was a child the last time she did this, standing by a brown river. Now the ocean is tossing the boat about. She likes it: the intensity of the new experience.

She places the rod back in the bag and fetches a burrito from below the deck. One of the sailors started preparing them as soon as the boat left the harbour. The burrito is included in the price of the fishing trip. She devours the soft, steaming roll, facing the open sea. Oil drips down her forearms and into her sleeves. Coriander gets stuck against the roof of her mouth. The sweet taste of chilli lingers in her throat.

The passengers on the deck look relaxed and relieved. They have left behind their routines today,

exchanging the straight asphalt lines of the city for the rolling water of the sea. Some of them come often, perhaps every Saturday. Paulina knows this from the way they take over the deck, like it belongs to them.

Close to Paulina, a group of passengers wearing near-identical windbreakers are drinking beer, the foam catching on their chins. They laugh loudly. They discuss how big the cod are here: huge, strong, and meaty. Paulina can't prevent a complacent smile when she looks at them. The feeling of solidarity lasts only a second. A woman's tipsy eyes rest on Paulina. Her lips pucker. Heads turn, and they go on talking quietly. With the back of her hand, Paulina wipes her cheeks, greasy from the burrito. Of course they can smell her difference. And there it is again: the shame, that old acquaintance she thought she had rid herself of, who has found its way back and — but actually, no, they aren't talking about her after all. Their eyes are directed somewhere behind her back. She turns her head quickly. Two young men are standing on the prow, the only black passengers on the boat. One is wearing a bright red quilted jacket, the other a green one. They don't have scarves, and their necks rise naked and thin out of the puffy jackets. They smile a lot and gesture enthusiastically as they speak.

Paulina can't help the relief washing over her. Relief doesn't come alone, though; it drags guilt behind it like a broken suitcase. She hastens to smile at the two men, the object of the other passengers' hostile looks, and stretches out her hand. The men are brothers and come from Cameroon.

We've lived here for a few years, one says.

A year and eight months, the other specifies.

Paulina nods, moved by the earnestness with which the first man hastened to correct his brother. Her eyebrows arch and her lips spread into a smile, as if effusive kindness could make up for the rudeness of others. The brothers don't seem to notice what's going on around them, though — or they don't care.

With renewed excitement, Paulina turns to face the sea. Petrol blue and steel grey. Gigantic clouds group together and disperse, their shadows following suit upon the water. She leans against the railing, her breasts pressing against the cold metal, to be as close as possible to the water. She isn't from here either. But she doesn't say this to the Cameroonians: that she moved to California three years ago. That during the first months she cleaned shopping centres, studied English, and planned her 'business'. She put aside as much money as she could. She walked from

one shop window to the other, looking at everything she would soon be able to buy. She would send some of the money home, of course; the bundles of bank notes would travel proudly across the Atlantic to the cottage, a validation of her departure; hurt feelings would be soothed. She bought a car and rented a house not too far from the harbour. Customers came to her like ants in search of honey. One of them, an old energetic man, gave his rod to Paulina. His overgrown nail poked her cheek as he commented how she was pale as dough, even anaemic, and that the sea would do her good.

Two hours after leaving the dock, the motor of the boat goes quiet; the ocean becomes louder. The Cameroonians don't manage to throw at first. The bait drops at their feet or rises too high in the air. Paulina takes the fishing rod from the bag, places the line against the handle with her index finger, opens the lock, bends the rod back, throws, frees the line, and watches the bait disappear into the water. Then she starts to reel quickly. She waits for the rewarding feeling of weight and thinks about the lottery. How much money is there in the can?

At least half an hour goes by before she feels a tug. The blue of the sea condenses. She doesn't have time to wipe the tears that the brightness squeezes out from her eyes. Her knuckles are white now, and the veins on the back of her hand swell as she reels the heavy catch. Suddenly the weight is gone and the rod swings back. The bait flickers and shimmers in the air, taunting her: Ha, and you thought you had it!

Around her, lines start to tug, first one and then another. The hands feel the weight and begin to pull, but no fish appear. The boat's captain paces up and down the deck and restrains the tourists: *Damas y caballeros, por favor*, he pleads. He taps their shoulders and orders who should pull and who shouldn't, to prevent everybody from tugging the fish towards themselves. The tangled lines try to detach. The men and women shout and push each other. They resemble the hippos that Paulina recently saw on Animal Planet, fighting for territory.

Finally, the tangled lines are cleared. Only the Cameroonian with the red jacket reels in his line triumphantly, his body leaning towards the sea until the surface of the water breaks and the fish bites at the light. The cod flies across the air towards the deck, eyes bulging in horror. The others aren't happy; everyone

feels the fish belongs to them. The woman who was drinking herself tipsy a few hours ago looks around, bewildered. The black kohl has spread under one eye like an exclamation mark.

What the fuck, that's my fish! she snaps.

Somebody places a soothing hand on her shoulder, but she slaps it away like she would a gadfly.

Stay out of this, Roddy, someone has to teach them how things are done, she barks. How you should behave *here*, she adds, and thrusts her hands on top of her hips, lifting her chin like the lessons are about to start.

The Cameroonian's hand doesn't shake when it holds the rod. The hanging fish's body glistens in the sun, turning first in one direction and then the other.

Paulina holds on to the railing. Her fingernails have the vestiges of scarlet nail polish, tiny stains at the top. Her hands are worn from continuous washing, and yet they always feel dirty. She takes quick breaths and tries to control the shaking.

She bends over the side of the boat like a branch snapped from a tree, squeezing the railing so hard the metal digs into the soft skin of her palms. Pungent, the chilli rushes to her throat. She gags until her stomach is empty and her mouth is filled with a sour taste.

She won't eat another burrito for at least a hundred years. She drops to the ground next to the cabin, pulls her knees to her breast, and leans her shoulder blades against the wall.

Even if she has only dozed for a second, something has changed. Then she notices it: at the bottom of the erstwhile empty cool box is a cod. It looks stupefied. Paulina gazes around her for the Cameroonians but they are somewhere on the other side of the cabin.

If she has the energy, she'll make a soup with the fish tonight. She and her strange companions will gather around the table to eat. They will discuss their day, what was in the news, and what the animals did in the nature documentary.

She'd already had the idea before moving to California. She'd heard that taking care of the elderly is a profitable business here. It's possible to earn 3,000 dollars per month, just for hosting one old person. That would never happen in her own country. Old people die at home, inside a house which generations inhabit together. If they aren't blessed with children — or if their children have heartlessly abandoned them in search of their own happiness — they die alone, God forbid.

34

But there were regulations Paulina wasn't prepared for. To register her house as an official elder care home, she needed to prove it had all the facilities and a certain amount of square metres. Her house was too small, the rooms too narrow. And what about those treacherous thresholds and stairs? Still, it was easy for her to find a way around the rules. Word spread and people began to contact her. Usually it was a husband and a wife who came, two siblings, or a widowed parent. Even if the adult children were holding gently on to the arm of the elderly, there would be something urgent in their eyes. Paulina invited them to sit on the porch. The way she held the porcelain coffee pot between her hands would make you think it was a trophy, as she told them how much care and love the residents would receive. The longer they sat and chatted, the more the confidence between them grew, its shape becoming as defined as that of the coffee pot, at the mouth of which, if light hit it at the right angle, you could distinguish a chink.

The money did not stream into Paulina's hands. Taking care of the elderly was not easy. And the fear of things going really wrong accrued in the corners of the house, much in the same way snails spread around a fish tank: one slimy centimetre at a time.

The lines whip through the air many times and then the last time. A thin cloud wipes across the sun. The boat heads back towards the harbour. The passengers sit on the deck drinking beer; a few doze under their caps. The Cameroonians look content. After a clumsy beginning, they started to catch fish like they knew exactly where in the dark sea they were swimming, the precise point at which they shifted their silver bodies.

Behind a plastic table on the deck, two sailors begin to clean the fish. Eyes, fins, tails spatter around. The hard wind does nothing to dispel the smell. The city is outlined against the sky. Paulina is never usually gone this long. It's been days since morning.

She places the rod in its bag and decides to give it to the man's children when they visit next. It's a good rod — it might have been very expensive or at least of sentimental value. The old man probably mistook Paulina for his daughter or granddaughter.

The sailors gut the fish quickly and Paulina gets her cod back — or what's left of it, that is: a hollow, torn trunk. From its grey underside the pale orange meat peeps out.

When the boat is close to the port, the sailor gives the lottery can to one of the Cameroonian brothers. He says something, maybe 'Oh wow' or 'Oh well'. He

shrugs and looks amused that it is he who caught the biggest fish.

The first noise tears the sky. Paulina, sitting curled up against the cabin, shades her eyes with her palms and tips her head to see. They are pouring down, dozens of them, maybe a hundred, squawking ravenously. Their white wings flap against the wind. Even though her neck is throbbing with pain, Paulina sits with her face up. There are so many wings that the sky is barely visible. The pelicans are gyrating in tighter and tighter circles above her. She scrambles to the cool box and covers the carcass of the fish.

Around midsummer, the fiancé of one of the girls paid her a visit from across the border. He arrived at the little cottage on the edge of the village. He knocked many times. Finally, he kicked the door down with his Nikes. He was received by silence. He sat on the couch and waited, holding a present for his sweetheart: a first-rate deodorant.

While he waited, he looked around and didn't like what he saw: the tables and the floor were covered with dust and there was a pile of dirty clothes on the armchair. The wallpaper was peeling off. Flies were feasting on the dining table. It smelled of rotten meat. Annoyance made his heart beat rapidly.

When he opened his eyes and saw the girl standing in front of him, he realised he had fallen asleep. She had a towel in a bundle under her arm and her red trainers were full of sand. The man thought that her face looked somehow distorted, until he realised it was smudged with makeup. Her hair was wet.

Have you started working in the circus? he snorted.

No. I swim now.

He laughed, but in a way that betrayed his irritation, and called his future wife a fucking duck.

She shrugged. To his shock, she started to hum. She took out a pack of cigarettes, shook it with a tiny hand gesture, and gave him a calculating look, as if deciding whether to tell him something. She lifted a cigarette to her lips but didn't light it. She hung the towel on the back of a chair and straightened it carefully. The gesture said: If only you knew. But the man didn't know. He took a lighter from his pocket, flicked it alight, passed the flame towards the girl, and said softly: Come here. His arm did not drop as the flame flickered between them.

In the evenings, once they were done practising, the girls roamed the streets of the village. Their tracksuits made whooshing sounds as one leg brushed the other. They didn't speak to anyone. One of the girls carried her towel over her back like a cape, holding her face high, the piercing at her nose gleaming proudly. Another one wrapped her towel around her neck, capturing her black fluttering hair, and stroked it the way she would a mink fur. Sometimes they opened their jackets to stretch the shoulder straps of their swimming suits, making them slap arrogantly against their skin.

They stormed inside the tavern and ordered large portions of meat and French fries. They gorged quickly, faces glinting with grease, expressions focused yet blasé, and left as soon as they were done.

At the cigarette factory, too, their behaviour had changed. They made a lot of mistakes which they didn't apologise for. More Cheap Whites disappeared during their shifts than at other times. They stretched their lunch breaks. They sang. One of them got yet another tattoo — a shamelessly visible stain above her shoulder blades.

All this raised suspicion of course, and the girls began to be watched. But they were always at the river, always together, and the only thing that seemed to interest them was the impact of water on the movements of their bodies. They were seen sitting on the muddy shore, content like piglets, shaving their legs while soap flew merrily around them. The locals viewed them as harmless, if somewhat unbalanced, so they were left alone.

Meanwhile the sky grew cold, the chimneys spat smoke, and the river wrinkled.

Water polished the girls' skin the way the sea washes shells clean in its tides year after year, smooth and hardened. Off came everything redundant and hindering, breasts included. Still, the girls struggled to get rid of their weaknesses: their small lungs, their hasty

need for oxygen, and their fear of the dark bottom water.

One morning they succeeded: they sank to the riverbed and remained there. Their bodies curled. It was quiet and dark. They watched the shadows and lights oscillating above. They forgot the need to breathe and talk. There were no pearls in these shells. They remained there, without moving, until even the river forgot them.

SANDRA, THE
PYRENEES

Sandra gets into the man's car. She chooses the back seat; the front would be somehow too intimate. Through the rear mirror, she notices the scar on his face: a pale red line from forehead to lips across the left eye.

My name is Sandra, she says after they have been driving in silence for a while.

Gustave, the man grunts and stretches his hand towards the back seat without taking his eyes off the road. The hand is surprisingly small for such a large body.

Thank you for stopping.

Gustave does not answer or look at Sandra. She is

just another piece of luggage riding in the back seat. She hopes he did not get offended about her informal way of addressing him. The French are so sensitive about these things.

His head, sparsely covered with patches of brown hair, moves slightly. The sun has burnt the bald spots and the skin is peeling. His sunglasses look strangely thin for such a wide face. His red Coca-Cola t-shirt is too tight.

Suddenly his back starts to shake and he chuckles: *Thank yoo.*

Sorry?

Thank yoo, that's what you said. *Thank yoo* and *stouping*.

After chuckling for a while, Gustave becomes serious and says: We have a long journey ahead of us, *mademoiselle*. I hope you're not easily car sick, the road is winding.

I'll be all right, Sandra snaps.

Okay then. I'll drop you off in the next town. From there on you'll have to figure out something else.

That's fine.

Iz it fine? Gustave turns his face towards the backseat, his mouth and eyes filled with mirth.

Sandra looks for an answer, something witty

to say, but she is afraid her French will just amuse Gustave further. She crosses her arms across her chest and stares, stubbornly, at the landscape.

Gustave sneezes and the laughter is gone.

The houses become scarcer and disappear behind the hills, which soon deepen into mountains. Sandra has never seen mountains before. They are amazing. The farthest ones are deep green-blue, the colour of a lake, even if nothing seems to flow or ripple in this hot landscape. Her quicksilver eyes take on their colour.

Gustave stretches his arms and leans backwards so that his seat pushes against Sandra's knees.

Now the landscape is made of yellowing meadows on one side and a thickening forest on the other. Grassland slides down the valley; forest climbs up the mountain. Sandra wipes her sweaty face with her shirt, and quickly smells her armpit. She closes her eyes and imagines she's already there, in the big city.

When she opens her eyes, she notices Gustave staring at her through the rear-view mirror. He has said something; the raised eyebrows reveal the question. He places his sunglasses in the cup holder.

Why are you carrying such a big bag with you? he repeats, impatient. His voice is hard, and it bends into laughter when he adds: Looks like you are on the run.

I'm moving. To Paris.

He raises his eyebrows. To *Parrhis*! Ambitious then.

Yes, Sandra sighs, trying to hold on to her smile despite feeling increasingly annoyed. I need a change, she says, pronouncing each word extremely carefully. She scratches the purple polish of her fingernails. Pieces of it rain down on her thighs, which are bare beneath a pair of blue shorts.

Well that is some change, Gustave says and rubs his eyes, looking bored.

Sandra blows her fringe aside and looks at Gustave intently, but he seems to have lost interest. Now it is Sandra's turn to stare: she lingers on his scar. It divides his face neatly in two. He notices her gaze and responds to it with a fierce look. Her face flushes. She is just about to turn her eyes away when he lifts a finger to his forehead and runs it, very slowly, along the scar.

A blind lion did this, Gustave says when his hand is back on the wheel. Suddenly his voice is low and solemn.

A lion?

My old man was one of those, you know, exterminators. He would drive from one customer to

the other, pesticide equipment and all. One couple, both of them circus animal trainers, hired him to get rid of ants in their house. I went along with him. The house was big and white, like a castle, you know, and there was a lot of colourful stuff growing in the garden. We waited.

He slows the car down and crouches over the wheel as the branches of big chestnut trees claw the windshield.

A guy came to greet us, walking a blue-eyed lion which he closed in a big cage next to the swimming pool, Gustave says. A woman, the man's wife I guess, waved at us from the balcony.

Every now and then Gustave lifts his face to see Sandra through the mirror, like he's weighing the effect his words have on her.

They went inside the house, the guy and my old man, he says. I wanted to stay outside.

The treetops from both sides of the road form thick greening arches. Their large leaves do not let any light through.

Didn't the lion scare you? Sandra asks. All of a sudden she is cold, despite the heat.

Scare! No, she was amazing. She was the most beautiful animal I'd ever seen.

His words boom in the car, dark in the leafy umbrage. Suddenly he seems to remember something that softens his face. Light floods the road and washes over an army of orange flowers, gleaming the way only mountain flowers do.

I saw all kinds of things with my father. But none of the animals were as beautiful as that lion.

His voice is even louder than before when he says: I just couldn't help it. *Stay on the porch*, they said, but I had to go to her. Real close. He uses his thumb and index finger to show how close to the lion he had dared to go.

Sandra nods vigorously to show she understands the significance of what he is telling her. She feels sticky. Tree roots bulge out of the road, causing the car to bounce. Some leaves are burnt yellow by the sun, and they make Sandra wonder whether the trees in Paris turn red in autumn and —

I can't really see with my left eye!

Sandra refocuses her gaze on the front mirror. When observed carefully, the surface of his left eye seems cloudier than the right one.

Isn't it difficult? Isn't driving, for example, difficult … with one eye?

Just then, the car reaches an abrupt curve, and

Gustave serenely steers the wheel, making it turn very softly.

All my other senses have sharpened, he says. I hear, taste, smell better than before. When I'm in the forest, I can even hear all kinds of little animals, far away.

There are no more flowers beyond the trees, but instead a bleak, rocky hill coloured by lichen. The hills radiate a heat which condenses inside the car.

I was supposed to take over the company, after my old man died. But it wasn't my thing.

And now you …?

I drive.

The road pulls itself into a straight line, and Gustave's grip on the wheel relaxes, his hands barely touching the brown plastic. Despite the open window on Gustave's side, the car smells of perfume and sweat. It smells of the two of us, Sandra thinks, and pulls the hem of her shirt down. The torn, fake leather of the seat makes her thighs itch.

How come you're all alone? Gustave asks suddenly, as if this detail has been bothering him.

As I said, I'm moving.

But all alone, and such a young woman, all kinds of bad things can happen, he says. Then he points his

49

thumb at his chest and declares cheerfully: You're very lucky *I* saved you.

Sandra is thrown back when the car drives over a big hole. Her hair glues onto her cheeks. Leaning against the front seat, she notices what's lying next to Gustave. She opens her mouth, but her voice is stuck in her throat. It must have been hidden under the magazines when she got into the car, or maybe it had always been visible, lying there naked, a third traveller. The blade isn't that of a little knife but some sort of scythe.

The car mounts higher, advancing increasingly slowly. Down in the valley the fields are tiny. Gustave holds the wheel with one hand and with the other, groaning, rummages for something in a plastic bag. A water bottle appears in front of Sandra. She grabs it stiffly. She doesn't look at the blade next to him, but it thrusts into her field of vision: a crescent shining in the undernight of the front seat.

She takes a tiny gulp. Most of the water streams down her chin. She locks eyes with Gustave through the mirror. Sweat makes his scar glow.

Thank you.

You were thirsty, he chortles, taking the bottle. He drinks, his eyes on the road, lips protruding like those of a child.

The car stops suddenly. They are now completely away from the forest. The sunlight is falling on a few fruit trees that stand proudly against the mountain wall.

Gustave stretches his arms clumsily and sighs: What a drive.

Unlike before, he doesn't look for her face in the mirror. Instead, he turns his head slightly towards her, but not enough for their eyes to meet. He only moves the pupil of his right eye.

Let's stretch our legs a bit, huh? he says and yawns, but it all seems rehearsed. He stumbles out of the car but does not, to her surprise, grab the knife. He takes a few steps. He fingers his pants and Sandra hears a relieved moan and the sound of urine splashing on the ground. Then he turns to the car, bends down, and picks up the knife.

She was right. The object isn't a simple knife; its blade forms an arc. There are no birds, no wind. Gustave knocks on the half-open window. She tugs at the belt. Her damp fingers slide down, then: click. She opens the door, stumbles out. The gravel road is burning. Sweat drops blurs her vision.

Suddenly Gustave flings the blade up. He uses it to dig something from under a nail and then wipes it with his shirt. He stops for a while just to look at

the landscape, squinting. Then he approaches her. He walks next to Sandra, then past her. The blade turns.

A tree shivers and a round, glowing object falls into his hand.

Take a bite, he says, and hands it over to her.

She looks at the orange in her hand. She digs her teeth into it.

Gustave laughs, a deep roar, and asks: Is that how Parisians eat *orrhanges*?

Late one night, the quicksilver-eyed girl returned to the river. She kneeled, relieved, to pick up the goggles from among the cold stones. With a swift hand gesture, she tucked them into her pocket, and was about to sprint away when she turned, for the last time, to look at the river. Leaves and boughs moved across the surface. Only the moon, white and round like a peeled apple, stayed put in the dark rushing water.

The next day, there was no one at the river, only the trees spreading their branches. The autumn sky was dark and low. The girls were in the village getting ready to leave. Their breath steamed. They pushed plastic bags, with goggles and towels peeking out, into the boot of a car. Then they squeezed inside, one on top of the other. The villagers observed how they organised themselves laboriously, so that everybody fitted inside with not one leg or arm sticking out. The one they called Adidas hurried the others. Urgency had been growing in her since new gifts had arrived from the place where her shoes came from. Now she sat with her hands ready on the wheel. The doors closed. The car powered away, past the villages and forests and fields, all the way to

the city, where the river appeared again from behind the factories and the war memorials, holding the city on its lap.

When the girls arrived at the Captain's sport complex, they went straight to the swimming hall. The legs of the swimming coach almost buckled when he turned to look at the newcomers: they carried the plastic bags and brushed their messy hair with their fingers. Their tracksuits were dirty. They wore rubber boots, or sandals, from which socks gushed out. Their fingernails were black. One of them was wearing glasses that made her eyes huge and idiotic and slow-blinking, like those of a cow. There were a lot of bones and flat chests. They grinned foolishly.

Though the coach didn't hide his contempt, the girls were glowing as they gazed around. The swimming hall was turquoise and vast, and outside its windows spread the playing fields and auditoriums. Since nothing is as beneficial for both financial profit and national pride as sports, The Near Side of the River has a sports complex of which the neighbouring countries can only dream. It's a mystery how such an amazing complex can stand on a piece of land that is but a black dot on the map. But there it is. The auditorium can fit as many people as any football stadium of a European capital. There is a five-star hotel, a living complex for the players, and a football school for children. There are also tennis courts and running tracks. And an emptiness: the best

players leave as soon as they are old enough.

The Captain's sports complex is best known for its footballers, but also for its boxers and runners. Not so much for women athletes and water sports: the pools are calm, the reflections of the ceiling unbroken.

The girls closed themselves in the changing room, where they peeled off their tracksuits, the harsh light exposing their exhausted bodies. They leaned towards the mirror. One of them took off her piercings, and carefully put them inside a matchbox. With shaking hands, they styled their hair so that not one strand could escape. The hair pins, glittery and as big as spoons, fastened with a click. The nose clips flattened their nostrils. Then the girls stepped into the hall, chins up, just as they had seen on TV. Even the short-sighted one walked straight and assertive. They stopped at the edge of the pool; the electric blue took hold of their reflections. They looked at the chipped tiles and the rectangle of tamed water, which once upon time was probably filled with promises that had now faded into only a hint of past glory. They jumped, for the first time, into water that didn't belong to the river. Chlorine wooshed into their eyes and ears. Each toe and hair and mole and scar was perfectly visible in the clear water. The tallest of them raised her tattooed arm, whistled, and they began.

They buoyed up to the surface, then swirled in the water

like ducks. Six feet whipped the air, then disappeared. Twelve feet started bending in step, accelerating and splashing until they ceased to be feet. As the bodies swung into somersaults, their bottoms flashed like mussels. Five pairs of hands threw one body horizontally into the air. The girls gathered in a circle which turned, first slowly and then quickly, growing in strength. Their eyelids and hair were covered in a thick layer of glitter, which made them sparkle. Kohl tears ran down their cheeks.

The coach didn't wipe his face, wet from the splashing water. Watching the performance — mesmerising despite its flaws — he felt his blood course through his limbs and penis, reinvigorating it to the point of rigidity. Suddenly the water of the pool looked promising to him, too.

A few months later, the girls posed for a photograph. They stood in a row according to height. Hands on their hips. Hip bones protruding forward defiantly. Their hair flattened by water and pulled tightly back, enhancing the furrowed foreheads that did not quite match their grins. They were wearing so much makeup that at a quick glance their faces looked identical, but after close inspection one could tell that each was terrified in their own way.

The photo was printed in the newspaper under the title:
TEAM OF SYNCHRONISED SWIMMERS FORMED BY GIRLS OF CIGARETTE FACTORY.

BETTY, SAN MARTIN

The casino smells of bedrooms in need of airing. Unsmiling girls are handing out drinks and cigarettes to the customers at the bar.

I hesitate for a second as I change the last of my money for chips. They are heavier than I had imagined. The dealer, a small black man, starts to shuffle the cards. The only players other than myself are two tourists I met at the beach: Magnus from Germany and Jeanne from France. Both have sunburnt faces. Jeanne calls over the waitress, who dashes to the bar as fast as her miniskirt lets her and soon returns with a turquoise drink.

Judging from the expressions on their faces, I'm not the opponent Magnus and Jeanne were hoping for. I try to hide my shaking by crossing my hands

over my lap. I check the time: Pappa will be here in two hours.

Magnus has drawn the highest card. He immediately raises, and Jeanne and I call. When the dealer turns over the first three cards on the table, the corners of Jeanne's mouth lift cheerfully.

Jeanne, you're a bad player, Magnus laughs.

Jeanne's face, draped with angularly cut hair, flushes even redder than before.

I win the first hand with three tens. Arranging my chips into neat piles, I say: I've been on this island for a month now.

A month … Jeanne mumbles. As soon as she gets her cards, she covers them with her palms.

I've been here for a week and I don't think I could stay for another, she says. I'm leaving after tomorrow.

Magnus looks at her, amused, and sighs: You're breaking my heart.

If I could decide now, I'd never have come here, I say.

Why did you come then? Jeanne asks.

It's a long story … because of a dog, actually. A Doberman puppy.

I expect intrigue, but both have fixed their eyes on the dealer's fingers, turning over the cards. Magnus looks excited and raises. I forget to breathe when the

dealer reveals the fifth and final card. Magnus shows his two pairs but, instead of looking at the cards, he looks at Jeanne and smiles.

I do not tell them how difficult the first months in Bucharest were. When I moved there last spring, I thought it would be easy to start a new life. But by the time I met Lux, I was stealing fish heads from a restaurant's garbage disposal.

I say: Last spring, I moved to a new country, and lived alone, a complete foreigner, until I met a man called Lux. I moved in with him right away. He sold phones that arrived through his mailbox in brown packages from I don't know where. I turned out to be a good saleswoman and the business started to grow; the apartment was filled with phones.

I sip the drink Magnus has ordered for me. The third hand starts. I look at Jeanne. Her expression is still bored. She taps her lower lip with a forefinger. The long, thin nail is perfect in its French manicure.

Fold, she says, and pushes the cards aside. She relaxes as soon as she is out of the game. She folds her hands behind her neck and leans back.

I try to read Magnus' face for information. Will he try to bluff this time? The trace of white fuzz under his nose is quivering.

I hastily continue: Soon, our business was so successful it made people jealous. One evening, when we got home from the kebab shop, the apartment had been burgled. The thieves had taken the only thing we had, the phones. So we got a Doberman to guard the flat. The problem was that we didn't know a thing about dogs.

Poor dog, Jeanne mutters.

I know! But the breeders who sold us the puppy promised to teach us how to raise it.

Magnus reveals a straight. I try to look relaxed, but I sit taut like a wick. These chips are all the money I have. If I lose, I'll never leave the island. The dealer collects the cards and starts to shuffle.

Whenever Lux and I weren't busy with the phones, we drove to the suburbs where the dog breeders lived, I say. The place was crawling with Dobermans. We drank beer and watched TV; we had nothing else to do. After the burglary, the phone sales started to drop.

Fourth hand now. The casino is starting to fill up. A new player joins us: she is a chubby woman with white curls, a revealing neckline, and flashy rings. She is from some northern country. My fingers ooze sweat as I grab the cards. Magnus has already raised, as always. He whispers something to the newcomer, probably about me.

So, black-market work and dogs! Jeanne snorts.

Yep, I say.

I am bathed in sweat. Even my underwear squelches against the chair. The newcomer only raises on the last round, the river. When she wins, her arm scrapes the chips like they are board-game pieces.

Let's continue, children, she says.

I know she's talking about the game, but I continue my story: One day, a friend of the breeders came to the house. He was happy and enthusiastic. He had just arrived from Saint Martin. The guy announced to us that in Saint Martin there's work for everyone! The rest of us just listened without interrupting. You leave poor but you come back, if not wealthy, at least wealthier, he said.

Jeanne giggles. Magnus' face is also joyful, and he orders more drinks. The dealer yawns theatrically while shuffling.

The decision to leave happened on a whim, I explain. That same evening, Lux and I counted our savings from the phone sales. There was enough for one plane ticket and the beginning of a new life in Saint Martin. We decided I'd go first.

I get out of the sixth hand as soon as I have seen my cards. My bad luck is getting worse. I learned

to play Texas Hold 'em long ago, before moving to Bucharest. We used the smallest coins as chips. At first I thought the game was called Texas, Hold Them!

Why do I always have such shit cards! Jeanne moans.

Magnus pats her leg encouragingly, like you would the hind of a slow but beautiful horse.

I tell them how I travelled from Bucharest to Paris with a truck driver who was a friend of the breeders, and then flew here from Paris. Everything started going wrong the moment the plane landed. The man who the breeders promised would greet me was not there.

Jeanne sighs almost empathically.

Poor sweetie, the old blonde says coldly, and pushes a heap of chips into the pot. She is already getting bored. She raises recklessly and gazes around, fishing for a different kind of catch. I'm sure Pappa would like this piece of Nordic flesh, even if she's ancient.

I looked for a cab and asked the driver to take me to the cheapest hotel possible, I tell them, as I size up the Scandinavian with a stare. The place he took me to wasn't a hotel. There was a row of little huts. In front of them was a swimming pool, but it was filthy. I

had to pay a deposit of five hundred euros, but I didn't mind. I was sure I'd earn the money back quickly.

From the disbelief on their faces, I realise they have rooms in tidy hotels, probably by the beach.

I look at my remaining chips. I try to steady my voice as I say: As soon as I woke up the next morning, I went for a walk along the road. I was sure it would take me some place where I'd find work — a port, restaurants, bars, hotels.

Magnus shakes his head again and I am sure it is because of his cards, but he says: I don't believe you! I'm sorry to say this, but … only a crazy person does that.

Magnus has three sevens, I have a pair of fives, and Jeanne has something she claims to be a straight, but it turns out that she miscounted the cards. The blonde feigns hesitation for a while before revealing her cards: three jacks and a pair of nines, a full house. Magnus looks at her with disbelief and curses.

The woman laughs: Have fun playing, kids. Then she gathers her chips and waddles towards the bar.

So rude, Magnus scoffs.

The ninth hand begins. I take a peek at my cards — they are shitty.

I don't know how long I sat by the road for when a car stopped, I tell Jeanne, as Magnus is busy ordering

his chips according to colour. Suddenly an old, worried face looked at me from the driver's window. The voice asked *Are you all right?*, and before I could answer, the door opened. I could feel the air conditioning. The driver spoke English with a strong French accent. *Come inside, for God's sake, and don't be afraid.* I sat on the cool seat. It was lovely.

Come on, show your cards already, Jeanne says after revealing her queens.

Don't worry, you win, I mutter, disappointed at her blatant disinterest.

Magnus yawns. I'm scared he will take his stack and leave.

Then we started chatting! I say, with a high-pitched voice. The man scolded me for being there on foot. He pointed to a guy walking at the edge of the road, who was clearly high and had a shiny object under his belt. I promised I'd be more careful. Every now and then he pointed his thumb at himself and said in a fatherly way *Pappa this* and *Pappa that*, and that's what I started calling him.

I sip the bubble-gum-flavoured vodka, hoping I'm not boring them. I can clearly see Pappa now, as if he were in front of me.

He began taking me around the island every day. Sometimes we drove to the beach. He urged me to swim while he sat on the sand watching. When I came out of the water my skin was white with salt; you could barely see the inky patterns of my tattoos. Like a fish in water, Pappa joked, pleased, as I wrapped myself in a towel. One day, he drove us to the casino. Christmas lights hung from the palm trees, pale in the sun, and the hotel and the casino stood side-by-side behind the trees. The hotel was quiet, its windows closed, but when we returned that evening, the building had woken up. Men, locals and tourists, went in and out of its doors. In one hotel window I saw a woman tussling with the curtain, which was possibly stuck or something. She was wearing a thong and I could see a man waiting for her on the bed.

I swallow many times to get rid of the bad taste in my mouth. The tenth hand is over. Magnus turns to look at Jeanne, who has put her hair in a bun over the nape of her neck. He places his hands on the table, ready to get up.

I think I've had enough, he says. Jeanne, you have no choice, I invite you to dinner. How do fried shrimps sound to you?

One more game, I squeak.

I'm tired, honey, Jeanne says surprisingly gently, and tousles my hair.

There you go, Magnus says, visibly content.

But don't you want to know what happened next? I ask, pleading.

The eyebrows of the dealer rise. Magnus gives Jeanne an impatient glance.

One more hand, Jeanne agrees.

The dealer starts shuffling the cards, not at all sluggish despite his night-long shift, but with swift gestures.

Well, tell us then, Magnus barks.

Once, when we were driving downtown, Pappa invited me for a drink in this casino, I say quickly. He was very proud of the casino, and of the hotel, too, you know, like he owned both. He told me that men pay a lot for a little fun in the hotel, and he was sure I'd learn the job easily.

Jeanne seems bewildered: Oh god, how disgusting!

I realised then that I *had* to leave this island, I say. But to buy the plane ticket, I needed the deposit money back. I found the landlord in one of the huts watching TV. He got awkward when I asked for my money. *Tomorrow*, he promised. He said the same thing for three days.

The dealer turns three cards face up: ten of diamonds, ten of spades, queen of spades.

I say: Pappa came every day. But I pretended to be sick while I tried to figure out how to escape.

Fold, Jeanne says.

It's just me and Magnus in the pot now. Magnus checks and I do the same.

The dealer turns the fourth card on the table: a jack of clubs. The lamp above the table blinks but the light does not go out.

Magnus bets coyly. I call.

The dealer turns the fifth card over: an ace of diamonds. The dealer glances at me: he has done his part. I feel dizzy, the chair jerks, I thrust my elbows on the table so as to hold fast.

The ace makes Magnus beam with confidence, like he has already won, and he goes all in. The piles of chips fall and spread.

I snap-call the bet with my last chips.

As expected, Magnus has a straight. He crosses his arms all puffed up and looks at me.

Not bad, Jeanne mews.

I show my full house: three aces and two tens. Jeanne's tipsy eyes home in. Magnus looks like he is about to choke and barely manages to swear: Goddamn …!

The card game is over. I say goodbye to my new friends, collect the pot which is my ticket out of here, grab my suitcase, and leave quickly before Pappa comes.

The airplane tilts and hurtles between two mountains up in the sky. I pull the blanket up to my chin and close my eyes. I do not even worry that I only have eighty euros remaining after having paid the dealer his share. Somehow, I'll get to Bucharest from Paris. A friend told me you can find low-cost flights all the time.

When I wake up, I am already in another country. At Charles de Gaulle, nobody speaks the same French as Pappa. When I ask the clerk, incredulously, if the ticket to Bucharest really costs 190 euros, she starts to lose her patience.

Mademoiselle, she says, the price of the ticket doesn't get any lower. Will you buy the ticket or not?

What about low-cost?

The clerk doesn't bother answering. Her eyes move to the next customer waiting in line.

I stand in the middle of the hall wearing the same summer clothes I had on when I left the island. After a while, the price of the ticket is 210 euros. As I lift my suitcase, I notice it has become very heavy.

People refuse to look at my stretched-out hand. They're busy, they have a lot of luggage and children, and travelling makes them nervous. But my hand is bold and resolute, it thrusts itself in front of people and forces them to slow down. The security guard apologises before ordering me to leave the hall.

The cold immediately enters my bones. If Pappa was here, now I'd go with him. Suitcases rush past me over the frosty asphalt. The doors of taxis slam shut. A soft voice grazes my ear:

Hey, what's your name?

Betty.

I've come far, too, you know.

He has pulled a hood wide over his ears. His cheeks and the tip of his nose are red. His lips are so chapped they look like scars. He tells me that he knows how it feels to travel alone and penniless. His smile becomes sad when he says: My family misses me too. Betty, I heard you say inside there that you're on your way to Bucharest. Turns out I'm going there too. I'm sorry you haven't managed to buy a ticket.

Get to the point already, I snap.

The thing is this, Betty, if you help me, I can help you. I'll pay whatever you need to get on that plane if you run an errand for me.

Help how? I ask, wiping my eyes and nose with my sleeve.

He raises his hand. His fingers are holding something in the air.

Candy, a gift for my folks, he explains.

Then he points with his foot towards a plastic bag, where I see clothes and more candy.

If there's space in your luggage, I'll be forever grateful, he says as he pats his backpack: Mine is completely full, as you can see.

I shift my weight from one foot to the other. I am hot and cold at the same time. Then I laugh so hard my stiff face tightens.

Yes, yes I can do that, I say.

Together we pack the bags into my suitcase. Then we just smile at each other in gratitude, until we notice that we should hurry if we want to catch the flight. We step into the brightly lit hall.

He disappears through the security check. I go to the counter where I am just in time to buy a ticket. I will have thirty euros left. I will return, after all, a winner.

Despite the fabulous sports complex that The Near Side of the River has, its athletes don't get to show their skills to anyone except their own countrymen. But, if they are good enough, they cross the bridge to the neighbouring country on The Far Side of the River, where they get a new passport and membership to a sports club that is internationally recognised. Sports is important on both sides of the river: a fragile link between two countries looking away from each other. In fact, in international competitions, the athletes of one side carry the flag of the other, and even sing their national anthem.

The girls arrived in the country they had thus far seen only as a bushy landscape behind the river bank. The city smelled of snow melting under car wheels, and of exhaust fumes and chestnuts cooked in huge pans in the middle of the street. Unlike at home, the chimneys of the factories did not puncture the horizon; instead, rows of sturdy, rough apartment blocks pushed the sky up further. The girls recognised the McDonald's from afar, even if they had never visited one before.

They walked, the burger wrappings rustling in pace with the snow under their shoes, making them advance slowly, tip-toeing between excitement and anguish. They ended up in a park, where they greeted the stony face of an exiled poet. The snow was mostly grey and yellow. Only the cathedral boasted a clean white. Next to the cathedral, a scrawny dog was sniffing the frozen core of an apple.

From that day on, the girls' view of the country that now owned them was limited to the windows of the swimming hall: first, new layers of snow one after the other; then, when the snow melted, a faceless street corner. What happened inside the swimming hall was all that mattered. For the first time, this side of the river would be part of the Synchronised Swimming Championship, and all because of the girls who had stretched their languid bodies on a river bank not so long ago.

The coaches stood by the pool, stone-hard determination on their faces, shouting when one toe pointed in the wrong direction. The toe straightened quickly. Insubordination would be a sign of disloyalty, so the girls did as they were expected. They tore their legs into splits even more impressive than before. They made propellers out of their hands. Their bodies became masts rising above the water's surface. The smallest of them was thrown into the air, darting like a cannonball, at which point she

would spread her arms and legs like a five-pointed star. The black swimming suits changed to canary yellow. A music compilation was put together for them, a balance of classical and modern music with some local folk melodies, during which they ploughed across the surface of the pool.

In the evenings, when they fell on their beds like lumbered trees, the girls felt the movement of water inside their bodies. It rocked them to a place that belonged neither to this nor to that side of the river. The beauty of the threshold: on the other side of it, everything was still possible. Perhaps they were happier then, more complete and satisfied, than they ever have been or would be.

When the visas arrived, they were elegantly folded in between the girls' passports, like they had always belonged there.

NINA, ROME

6.15 am

Nina makes herself a quick breakfast in the kitchen and returns to her room, where she curls up in the still-warm sheets and nibbles at some bread. She looks at a black crucifix hanging on the wall, a framed map of Rome, and a metal shelf filled with Italian novels — her silent and meaningless companions. Her eyes stick to the titles like flies caught in glue. She springs from her bed, opens one of the books at random, and starts reading. She realises that not only the text but also her own thoughts are in a language that's not her own.

7.00 am

The customers pour out while Nina holds the café door open. Sentences do not glide past her but through her. Even people look different today. Now that the movements of their lips, the arches of their eyebrows, the expressions in their eyes, and the sloping of their shoulders chime with what they say, their features have sharpened. Nina orders a cappuccino, places her bag on the counter, and tastes the words in her mouth.

Tourist season starts soon, right?

The waiter rolls his eyes dramatically. Don't even mention it, he scoffs, banging the strainer against the sink.

Where I come from, there are no tourists, Nina says.

Oh, I thought you were from around here. From the south then?

No! Actually, I'm not Italian.

The waiter asks with casual surprise: Wow, where did you learn Italian?

Nina scoops the foam with her spoon and licks it, quickly, like wiping away a secret. She grins and tilts her head. The door is constantly opening and closing, the cups are chinking, somebody wants brown sugar.

She looks for an answer but only manages to laugh.

Her lips, which have grown accustomed to silence since her arrival in this country, now feel supple. Words do not come to her from the outside, but from within, whole and ready. The articles slip into their places effortlessly: they don't make her stutter, but drip from her lips. The endings of words, which are forever changing in her mother tongue, straighten. Diminutives, usually everywhere, fade.

The coffee is so strong. I just had one sip and I'm completely awake, Nina giggles.

She drinks her coffee like it's an espresso and orders another. A drop of sweat lingers on her temple. It's so easy to be here and pause the morning for a while. Now she can even recognise irony — Whatever you do, don't let your coffee get cold, miss, says the waiter — and she answers in the same way, making words circle around the intended message.

She leans her elbows on the counter, pushes her short hair back behind her ears, and fiddles with the empty cup. She is completely alert. She thinks that something is missing and soon realises it's shame. She places the bill under the cup and hurries to the bus stop.

8.15 am

Nina doesn't know much about what's going on at the warehouse, except for her own tasks. Valeria helped her get the job as a picker. The boxes handled by pickers contain drinks and food that stay unchanged for years: cheese crackers, sugary popcorn, crisps, and sodas.

She leaves her bag inside a locker marked with her name and puts on a yellow safety vest. She sees a glint of Valeria's red perm in the glass-walled office. Valeria is speaking intensely on the phone and does not see her. They will catch up later. Nina was lucky to meet her immediately after moving to Italy. Valeria helped her settle into Italian life, showed her around and told her what she needed to do to fit in. That was a month ago. Even if Valeria isn't from the same place as Nina, they share a mother tongue.

There is a constant humming in the warehouse: computers, air conditioners, lamps. The steel shelves rise like giants. The lamps aren't visible — their white light spills in between the ceiling and the uppermost shelves. The safety vest swishes as Nina pushes the cart towards the first shelf, the location of which is written down on the day's to-do list. Every time she moves, the safety vest reeks of years-old sweat.

There's nothing that I can't say in both languages, she thinks, and grabs the handles of the cart. Nothing stays inside one language. Each thought — like the one of how she will eventually grow numb to the noise and the smell of the warehouse — begets its double.

10.22 am

The delivery vans wait in the car park in sturdy silence. One has just arrived. The door opens and Angelo appears. He's the only driver who always greets Nina with a charming hello, which is why she now heads towards him, lips already prepared for an opening sentence. There is a naive excitement on her face as she asks: How are you today, mister Angelo?

He is focused on searching through his pockets and looks startled, as if this little woman has sprung up from under the asphalt.

Spring is here, isn't it, Angelo?

She can feel that new entity that is absent from her mother tongue, the copula: *to be*. How naturally it falls into place, like rainfall on a dry stream.

A lovely day! she says, panic now creeping into her voice.

A few darts of spittle land on Angelo's sunglasses. He straightens his back, smiles amusedly, touches his ponytail, and, as he jangles his keys, says in English: Very good miss, very good Italian!

The tattoo at the bottom of his neck moves. It's one half of a swordfish who has speared a hairy mole with its bill. Angelo swings the keys in the air, notices something, and starts walking towards it. There is a woman at the door of the warehouse. He lights a cigarette for her before doing one for himself. The woman takes the cigarette sulkily and glances at Nina.

Who's that?

Angelo gazes at Nina and snorts. He stretches his arms, the cigarette fuming skyward, and says: Ah, no one, just some Russki.

Like a flung stone, the word catches Nina off guard, almost toppling her over. He waves his hand high and smiles at her.

12.30 pm

Nina squeezes her way between the lunch tables to the back of the room, where Valeria and Mia are sitting. They both work in customer service. At the beginning, when Nina's back ached every day, they comforted her with prospects of a promotion. Some day, when Nina's Italian is fluent enough, she will sit in a comfortable chair and just answer the phone.

Valeria asks her: How are you, *amore*?

Since this morning, Nina has been waiting to tell them, her only friends, what happened. Maybe she will switch straight into Italian and share her news like it's nothing, let shock settle on their faces and then welcome their hysterical queries. Afterwards, when they have calmed down and digested the situation, they will start a new conversation in effortless Italian, the three of them, heads bent together in confidence.

I'm okay, Nina says in English, fiddling with her piercings. She smiles timidly, like a child in front of older playmates, and opens the plastic container with yesterday's leftovers.

The women nod encouragingly and return to Italian. Mia, who is from Naples, looks relieved, like she has dipped from a cold pool into a warm one. She

tells Valeria about the coming weekend trip home, pronouncing the last word dreamily, like it was not just a train ride away.

When Valeria unwraps her sandwich, the smell of ham bursts out and a wrinkle appears on the side of Mia's nose. Nina closes her container; the pasta is overcooked and the tomatoes watery.

12.45 pm

On the surface of it, it's a day like any other. Dust grows in the corners of the room with the first dead flies of spring. The sun isn't visible, but its light condenses on the surface of the vans and enters the room through the window.

Солнышко. Not sun, but little sun. Nina's lips form the edges of the word, rounding her mouth like a glassblower. The fact that her thoughts have been floating around in Italian for the whole day only now sinks in — but it comes back to her, her mother tongue, with that gentle, playful *solnyshka*. Unlike its Italian counterparts, the word implies a childhood sun that hisses as it sinks behind a river.

A very young woman stands in front of the draining board and empties an instant coffee sachet into a mug. The safety vest stretches across her enormous back, almost bursting at the edges, and squeezes under her armpits.

Mia leans towards Valeria and puts her hands together. Speaking of whales, she says, I don't know if you've seen our new employee yet. I hear she's the boss' niece and failed all her exams in Roma Tre.

Valeria's eyes are narrow as she frowns. Nina expects her to snap at Mia for her meanness.

That one is a real *p*——, Valeria says cheerfully, and looks at the girl who is now stirring her coffee. She beckons her to join them. The girl, insecure but content, walks towards them holding the coffee mug against her chest. Valeria notices that Nina is frowning at her, so she winks.

She's new here, she slyly tells Nina in Russian, who realises she has just been given an incomplete translation of the dialogue.

The expression Valeria used is Italian slang, harmless-sounding at first. Its meaning, which is only recognised by speakers of Italian, refers to overweight women. And if you change one letter, the meaning also changes, this time to a derisive word for vagina.

Nina carries this knowledge inside her now. It's like a stomach ache.

2.17 pm

If you forget to push the boxes through your legs when you lift, you might seriously injure your back. A box falls on the floor and its contents, tiny red soda cans, roll around in the buzzing white light. Nina picks them up slowly. Her mind is still humming with the inexplicable realisation that she can now speak Italian. Inside the office, she sees Valeria holding the phone between her cheek and shoulder. It pains her to realise that she doesn't know her after all, that the only one here who shared her language up until now is an entirely different person.

5.52 pm

The bar across the street from the train station is empty. The chairs and tables spread across the pavement, which is spotted with chewing gum. Nina chooses the chair closest to the road and slumps. Her

feet are throbbing. Her window is on the top floor of the building behind the bar. Going there now seems impossible, as if the person who got back from work yesterday and the person who is sitting here now couldn't occupy the same space.

A cluster of small lamps hang above the entrance of the bar. Their light blocks the waiter's face as he walks towards Nina. She orders a glass of house red, even if she would like a whole carafe. The waiter realises she doesn't want to chat and leaves her alone. She feels the presence of something superfluous, and notices that she's still wearing the safety vest. She pulls it off with one gesture, crumples it into a ball, and, without knowing what to do with it, places it under her chair.

A train dashes through the darkness and makes the evening hold its breath. The things around her no longer feel duplicated but interlocked. Wine is just grapes in a glass. The chasm between the two languages has disappeared, leaving space for something else that, for the time being, she can only anticipate. She takes a more comfortable position in her chair and puts her cold hands in between her thighs. Even if she dragged herself here like a wounded animal, she's suddenly so hungry that she's ready to sink her teeth into the

edge of the table. Instead, she gobbles all the nuts in the bowl and asks for more. She will just sit here to observe the trains and their passengers framed by lit windows, and guess whether they are coming or going.

On the street next to the entrance to the tavern, three little girls imitated swimming movements. They scooped the air, which smelled of sand and manure. Their necks craned and their mouths affected a photogenic smile. They were wearing tiny, neon-coloured shorts with patterned t-shirts that revealed their rapidly growing legs and arms.

Behind the children, the window of the tavern was blurry with dirt. It was time to turn on the TV. Beer flowed, the ashtrays filled up, and husks of sunflower seeds fell to the floor. The men sat quietly. The competition that was soon to be broadcast did not excite them in the way football did — it was, after all, just women in a pool.

Now, shh.

The TV crackled for a while before the image of the swimming pool settled on the screen. The tavern keeper's fingers, yellowed from nicotine, turned the volume up. A strange language could be heard as an echo under the commentator's voice.

The screen homed in on the colourful swimsuits,

the tight hairdos and the tense faces, identical in their makeup. Music filled the room, a place so far from the world depicted on the TV that it could have belonged to a different time altogether. Teeth cracked open the salty sunflower shells. Mouths made observations about the half-naked bodies.

Despite the feigned disinterest on the men's faces, their feet, stomping against the floor, betrayed excitement. Maybe the girls weren't the most beautiful and talented competitors, but they belonged to them, like the berries and fruits growing on their soil. Even if the other country had claimed them. And so they waited.

But their turn never came. Other girls, beautiful indeed, delicious in their colourful swimming suits, but foreigners nonetheless, appeared. The blue of the swimming pool dissolved into their empty beer glasses. The TV went quiet. A hand stubbed out a cigarette on the counter with a disappointed gesture.

The tavern keeper spoke first. Well that's that, he said, clearing his throat and grabbing a grey rag. He looked at it as if expecting confirmation.

Maybe they chickened out, said a half-blind man who was sitting right in front of the TV, gloating, with his hands protectively around his pint. And now they are

hiding, embarrassed, in a corner somewhere.

How does that saying go? With their tail between their legs …

A sudden slap put an end to the discussion and the faces turned to the tavern keeper, who had thrown the rag down.

Goddamn! he shouted. They escaped, don't you get it? And they aren't coming back, those wenches.

He had created the kind of silence that only people of his status can create. The faint outrage gathered like phlegm in the patrons' throats and then it was coughed away. The men rubbed their salty palms against their thighs and got up. The door of the tavern inhaled dust and slammed shut.

Two men loitered inside. They tucked their shirts in their pants, tied a dragging shoelace. As the tavern keeper disappeared into the kitchen, they assured each other, with the solemnity that comes after drinking, that there was an explanation for everything.

Maybe the girls won after all, one of them suggested. Then with more determination: And soon the whole world will talk about that victory!

Reporters will come here, the other added. They'll want to see where those missuses lived and swam. How great the land that raised them actually is!

On the street, the little girls were about to start their performance. They raised their arms into triangles and each lifted one leg up, preparing for a jump, like they had seen on TV. A small sandal slipped out of place.

That show was over, too, one of the two last drunkards leaving the tavern decided. He squinted his eyes; both the sun and the children's silly excitement, completely indifferent to anything around them, weighed on him. Off you go, he yapped at the girls, frozen first in alarm, then in anger. The foot returned reluctantly to the sandal. And then came the final sentence, loud and simple: Don't you have anything better to do, heh?

LIDIA, THE NEAR SIDE
OF THE RIVER

When the villagers hear I'm back, they come to me with food and wine, linen and towels. Only Bird Breeder comes empty-handed.

Even if my name hasn't been Lidia for years, here they still call me that. Lidia, have you started plucking your eyebrows? You do know they might never grow back? Where's your ring? Are you already forty, or older? Where were you when your parents died, Lidia?

I eat huge slices of pie filled with whole cherries and drink a mug of wine. One of the old women starts doing my manicure: aniline red on the edges and faded pink in the middle.

I answer their questions briefly and don't hide my yawns. A few more hours until sunset. The women aren't in a hurry, why would they be — so old already, they may as well wait for death here rather than at home. This is what they say as they make themselves comfortable in their chairs. Their curiosity is like their mouths: open, hungry, grotesque in their missing teeth.

When Bird Breeder finally arrives, the women leave, sulkily but swiftly. Old cunts, he mumbles after them.

He walks through the garden like he did years ago, without waiting to be invited. A faded shirt hangs from his thin, bent body. He sits next to me on the porch and nods a hello, as if the last time we met was yesterday. He doesn't look me in the eyes or ask questions. His silence feels more poignant than the women's inquisitiveness.

I fetch him a mug which I fill with plum wine. My mother used to serve the wine. The cups are the same, as is the floral morning gown that I found in the closet.

I can't help staring when he drinks, holding the mug with both hands. The shaking is slight but it puts the hands in a state of continuous restlessness,

as if they are trying to get somewhere. His fingernails are chipped.

He has raised doves for as long as I can remember. The birds fly incredible journeys around the world and always find their way back. The villagers laugh at him for it, some gently and some disparagingly. Bird Breeder doesn't care, he loves his doves, talks to them and trains them for competitions; he keeps them in a tall cage in his yard. But when people call his birds *pigeons* — then he intervenes. They are doves, not pigeons, he corrects them solemnly.

We stay silent. I lose sense of time, whole years disappear, until I notice the veins on my hands. I can feel beneath us how the porch, with its skewed rail and its rotten stairs, is trying to hold on to the house.

How are the doves? Do you still raise them? I ask.

He shakes his head. He searches for the words for a long time. Then: I still have my doves, but I don't compete anymore. The corners of his lips drop for a second, but when he continues his voice is full of pride: You know, before I quit, I won the first prize in the national dove competition. My birds were the best because I take good care of them. You know this, I crossbred them the proper way, gave them good food. After the competitions I would spoil them, he chuckles.

Why did you stop competing then?

The birds got old. It's expensive to do the crossbreeding properly. Ah, who cares. I never had much money anyway, he says.

I grab the wine bottle to refill his mug, but he lifts his arms to rebuff me and says: If you want, you can come and take a look at the beauties. He slurps the last bit of wine. Then he finally looks at me.

We walk slowly towards his house. We cross a dry stream and pass an abandoned dairy. I'm still wearing flip-flops and the morning gown, under which I can feel my stomach sagging. My eat-well regime was interrupted by the women plying me with their pies.

Bird Breeder walks strenuously, dragging his feet and breathing heavily. I hesitate to grab his arm — he would possibly find it humiliating. He wipes his forehead with a handkerchief he keeps tucked in his sleeve. He starts telling me about his new plan that will make him a rich man — rich and happy, he pants with a smile. He seems to be mumbling to himself, saying something about numbers and prices. A man made ten thousand a few years ago by putting up solar panels in his field, he says. Energy always sells, even during recessions.

I imagine him in the field surrounded by solar

panels, smiling, doves perched on his shoulders.

They're coming tomorrow to survey the property, Bird Breeder says.

Who? I ask.

Two men who are in the solar panel business. They need land.

Perhaps sensing my doubts, he adds: They're reliable guys. Young. Enthusiastic. They seem capable and they promised that everything will be in the contract. Everything will be done according to the rules.

He stops to catch his breath before adding: They come from The Far Side of the River. Then he points behind his back, as if the other country began just there, and concludes: Like anything new that ever comes to this godforsaken place.

I rub my eyes, which sting from yesterday's mascara. On the airplane I put my makeup on long before landing. As I was using the mirror in the tiny toilet, my eyelashes asked me: Who for?

We walk into the garden. Bird Breeder has always lived here, in a tiny house surrounded by dry land. There's nothing on his property except the house, a bird cage, and some peach trees. A long time ago I would pick up the peaches before they rotted, and in

return was allowed to stroke the birds. Their feathers felt oily and hid a cooing sound inside them.

The wind clatters the door of the outside loo. Next to the house, a loose wire whips the air. Bird Breeder walks straight to the biggest tree and the murmuring cage under it. He hands me a jug, which I know I must fill at the well. The water is brown but fresh.

A strong smell surrounds the cage. Bird Breeder is whispering to his pets, his face almost touching the bars with one palm on the floor, open invitingly. I give him the jug and he fills the troughs.

Water splashes on my toes. I must know, immediately: How do they find their way home from so far?

His eyes light up. He takes an excited breath, ready to discuss his favourite topic. Then he shrugs and sighs: I don't know exactly. But it has something to do with magnetic fields. It's a sure thing. It's been studied a lot.

He takes a plump bird from the cage and holds it right under his chin. The shaking hands don't startle the bird. It darts its black eyes.

They found poison, Bird Breeder states. In the groundwater of the river, in the gardens, inside the fish and the birds.

I remember hearing, a long time ago, that farmers here started to do better thanks to a new pesticide which was supposed to be applied directly to the soil. Then dead fish started to emerge from the river, belly up, and the birds began to lose their feathers.

But that was a long time ago, I say.

Bird Breeder shakes his head. Things don't disappear just like that, he says, and places the dove on my palm. I'm afraid of squeezing too hard. The bird thrashes about, eyes bulging with terror. I press it against the empty space of my chest. The dove stops moving. I suddenly have two breasts again.

Bird Breeder takes the dove back, puts it inside the cage, and closes the door. He turns to look at his land, perhaps picturing it radiant with solar panels.

The land surveyors are coming tomorrow, he says.

That's when it starts then, I say.

The next day, I return to Bird Breeder's house. First I see the white truck at the end of the muddy road. Bird Breeder is standing next to the field with two men from The Far Side of the River. They are wearing baseball caps. Their jeans are clear blue. Their teeth flash white when they laugh. One of them is tall and

thin. The other one is short but broad-shouldered. They nod and gesticulate a lot. They pat Bird Breeder on the back and hold his arms when he stumbles. When they notice me, all three wave eagerly.

Bird Breeder comes to me and suggests I sit by the table under a hunched parasol.

Have some iced tea, he says, nodding towards a metal jug.

Thank you.

He seems nervous and excited. Suddenly he remembers something and walks, mumbling, towards the house.

Maybe because of the sun or the overly sweet tea, the feeling of having returned sweeps through me. My body, until now tense and alert, relaxes. I look at the field, which has always stayed the same, yet is now changing. The taller man is standing behind some sort of camera on top of a yellow stand. The shorter is holding a notebook and walking among the hay.

I wish he would open my legs like he opens the hay. Soon he stuffs the notebook into his pocket. The other man lifts his face up from the machine. Time to eat! I help Bird Breeder set the table. The men have brought beer, which has been cooling in the well. The atmosphere is cheerful. We drink straight from the

cans. Bird Breeder seems younger. He asks about the size, the function, and the resistance of the panels. He seems clueless, but the two men are friendly and give him detailed answers.

Those panels, then, they suck the light in and turn it into electricity? he asks as he breaks bread.

The taller man takes a sip of beer and bites into an onion. He chews quickly and replies: Exactly! So the solar panels work in a way that they transform the radiation of the sun directly into electrical energy.

Unbelievable. Those thin boards, I say.

Isn't it? They're becoming very common. Luckily we realised their value in time, the shorter one says, blinking at me.

Indeed, who knows how long I'll be around, Bird Breeder says and makes the men laugh.

You youngsters are so capable, he adds. I can only wonder and try to follow. I'm too ancient for this.

Oh no, not at all! the shorter one hastens to say, grinning. You were wise enough to get into it.

Bird Breeder snorts in a way that shows he's not used to compliments but enjoys them.

And obviously any Peter the Peasant could thrust one panel up on his roof and have enough electricity to read lottery tickets, but with this space — the taller

one says, making a big arc with his hand holding the beer can — one can have dozens of panels. That is quite something, I think.

The shorter one nods approvingly. He cuts a tomato, spreads plenty of salt on the deep red halves, and adds: Maybe even one hundred.

More eager nodding. Teeth bite into onion, bread, tomato. A bright curved cucumber appears on the table. A new beer can hisses open — the most wonderful sound in the world. I gave up drinking in the States but different rules apply here, even for me.

The land surveyors are quiet for a while. Then the shorter one looks at me. Without saying a word, just letting his gaze move along my face, neck, and neckline. Suddenly I feel like laughing. Even if the gesture is vain, I bring my fingers to my hair.

Maybe later we would meet, the land surveyor and I. Maybe when I walk away from Bird Breeder's house, I would hear steps behind me. He wants a moment alone with me, hoping that I don't mind, and he would say so without expecting a reply, and then, as if by accident, his fingers would brush my hip, linger there, climb my defective side. When I let the dress drop to the ground, he would see my nakedness — the scar like the scream of a bird on my skin — and then

he would back off, disgusted.

So, I clear my throat. I press my fingers against the cool can. This is probably a very silly question, I say apologetically — but the men warmly encourage me to continue. How can one calculate the earnings from the panels? I mean, how can one tell how much energy they produce? Do they all have some kind of a meter or something?

The pals exchange gazes.

It's all in the contract, I suppose?

I turn to Bird Breeder, from whom I expect interest or at least some kind of survival instinct, but he's focused on dipping a slice of cucumber in the salt.

Finally the taller one says: An excellent question from Miss America! He swings his hand towards me, like a talk show host. His watch, a sturdy piece of silver, glints.

The shorter one smiles, relieved, and lets his friend explain how they would keep track of the panels directly from a reader in their office, in The Far Side of the River.

Bird Breeder says with earnest assurance: Everything is in the contract.

I open my mouth to ask something else, but Bird Breeder is now staring at me, and his eyes have a

severity that puts me back in my place. You've been gone for too long, the eyes say.

I let my shoulders drop and focus on the taste of the food. I missed the texture of freshly picked onions on my tongue. Honest and undisguised.

The men aren't in a hurry to return to work, but eventually they get up. They hold their hands awkwardly in the air, careful not to touch their jeans, not knowing what to do with them now that they've used them to eat. The notebook flaps comically from the shorter one's jean pocket. They walk slowly to the field, where the tall yellow machine stares into the distance like a neutral observer. The men exchange a few words. The shorter one glances at the house and spits.

I help Bird Breeder carry the dishes to the kitchen. He's tipsy. His face is glowing and he doesn't notice that his shaking hands are making the coffee spill.

Promising, right? He says, asking for my approval.

I nod vaguely.

Everything in the room seems old and stagnant, apart from the pile of papers in the middle of the table. Suddenly the presence of the two young men feels insulting. I hope the field swallows them. I look at Bird Breeder, whose bones protrude from under his skin. I feel a twitch in my stomach.

When he washes the dishes, soap water froths everywhere. His shabby brown trousers would fall if they weren't held by braces. He's wearing sandals and socks, one of which has gobbled the end of one of his trousers. It's this tiny detail, the end of the trouser inside the sock, which is why I need to leave right now.

First I walk quickly in fear the men might be following me. I keep on glancing behind my back but there's nobody. Even the shapes I mistake for people are only fruit trees, orange in the setting sun. I start slowing down. The heat hasn't left the ground — I can feel it against my flip-flops. There's no rush anymore. I think of the fresh onions and cold beer while walking to the house, very slowly now, as my flip-flops survey the land.

Dissonance — like after a long journey or at least — they

Disoriented — like after a long journey or a feast — they emerged from their hiding places. With no apparent sense of direction, they didn't seem to be heading anywhere in particular, one following the other past the fences and the utility poles and the faded signs taped on them, tottering and swaying along the bumpy road. They of course couldn't read the signs, and anyway were busy marking the territory — the street corners, the gates, the trunks of trees.

The rising sun shone over the forests and neighbouring villages; it washed over them, and over the cottages with their vegetable gardens, and the shop and the tavern which were scattered about like chess pieces after a game; over the blue roof of the monastery, the desolate factories, and the stony Lenins; the auditoriums, where empty seats looked out at the football field; stopping just short of the mute swimming hall.

The river streaked through the land. At some point it straightened and widened, gobbling up a few bushes, indifferent to borders. Here the dogs arrived, a bit tired now after their morning stroll. They were so thirsty they

sank into the water up to their bellies. Stones slipped under their paws. Water rinsed the dirt and the urine off their fur. They lay down in the grass, replenished and sated.

The grass was tall and dry:_one torn plastic flip-flop lay there, a shy reminder of absence. It had been a long time since anybody came to the river. The rusty yellow tractor was still on the riverbank, its excavator up in the air like an unfinished sentence.

The river flowed in a rush, chasing the bigger rivers that lead to the sea. There were no clouds in the sky. There was only the wide, dark stream of the river, and the dogs, who until now had been dozing, but, startled by a noise or a sudden movement, all at once opened their eyes. Darting glances, a musty breeze. After a few hesitating seconds they took off, tails up, teeth baring, pink tongues hanging out. They too were on a chase.

ACKNOWLEDGEMENTS

Thank you:

My editors Molly at Scribe, and Hazel and Jay at Book*hug Press.

Leenastiina at Rights & Brands agency.

And Carlos F. Grigsby: thank you for helping me with the translation and for showing me the rigours of short fiction.

The idea of the threshold, on page 73, is from Peter Handke's *Slow Homecoming*.